The Psalter Of John II

John M. Etheridge

Infinity Publishing

ISBN 0-7414-1728-6

Published by:

519 West Lancaster Avenue
Haverford, PA 19041-1413
Info@buybooksontheweb.com
www.buybooksontheweb.com
Toll-free (877) BUY BOOK
Local Phone (610) 520-2500
Fax (610) 519-0261

Printed in the United States of America

Printed on Recycled Paper

Published December 2003

ACKNOWLEDGMENTS

My help cometh from many sources and without it there would not be a book of psalms. My wife, Frances, has been wonderful help as a critic, an editor, and a cheerleader.

The Rev. Ned Bowersox, my Rector, has been tremendously supportive and has also done some editing. His most important contribution is his apparent universal approval of anything I write. His kind are always nice to have around. The Dunhams, Virginia (Ginny) and Bill, are almost as benevolent in their approval as the Rector, and do offer some very good suggestions, which are helpful.

My East Texas cheerleader and supporter is Dorothy Miller, a friend from High School who was really taken with Psalter I. She has been very helpful in her suggestions and creative critique.

My daughters and sons (in-law) never say anything other than WONDERFUL, HOW GREAT, and MARVELOUS, but it makes me feel good about what I have done.

To my great joy, the cover design was done by my number one granddaughter, Elizabeth Lloyd, an Art Major at The University of Texas, Austin of whom I am very proud, and grateful also.

And finally to the people at Templegate, especially Thomas Garvey for allowing me to build the cover design on the framework of the cover of the first volume of psalms, published by Templegate.

However the important thing is that you, the reader, find this volume helpful, and maybe bring you closer to our Lord; that is what He/She wants, so enjoy.

PSALTER OF JOHN II

INTRODUCTION

In early 1994, after a conference at Laity Lodge, a Texas hill country retreat center, I began writing psalms as a Lenten discipline. Our conference leader had been an expert on the Psalter of David, and in the course of the weekend she challenged us to write a psalm of our own. I accepted the challenge, and found a new way to pray and build on my relationship with God. I shared my psalms with my family and close friends who were impressed, and urged me not only to persist but also find a way to have them published. The good people at TEMPLEGATE PUBLISHING COMPANY agreed with my family and friends, and in November 1996 *THE PSALTER OF JOHN* was published. We were delighted with the overall appearance and layout of the book, and felt that Templegate had done a wonderful job. I was overwhelmed with the reception the book received in this community and dumbfounded at the reception it received outside my close circle of family and friends. The ink wasn't dry on the first printing when my Rector, Ned Bowersox, was pushing me to start writing again. Daily I still talk to God as if He were my best friend, and while I feel closer to Him, the problems we talk about have not changed that much. Lent 1997 is approaching so this may be a good time to start *THE PSALTER OF JOHN II.*

A lot of water has passed under the bridge since Epiphany 1997, including colon cancer, bilateral cataract surgery, Parkinson's Disease, and the day of infamy September 11, 2001, which brought us to Lent 2003. Psalter II has been finished for months now but until now I have been distracted by many other problems and just now getting around to preparing this for publication. One of my editors observed that this volume was not as joyous or carefree as Psalter I and that may be due to life's circumstances which generated many of the songs of praise and thanksgiving which are the primary elements expressed in Psalter II and Psalter I.

Another unpleasant occurrence was the death of my old friend, Hugh Garvey of Templegate Publishing Company. He was responsible for the very handsome, first volume of psalms, *The Psalter of John.* He lost his battle with cancer in January 2003.

As before, my suggestion is to read one of these songs of praise and thanksgiving, then think of what is being said, and pray that you will find yourself closer to God; I certainly was when they were written.

Corpus Christi, Texas

The Psalms

THE PSALTER OF JOHN II

Psalm 1

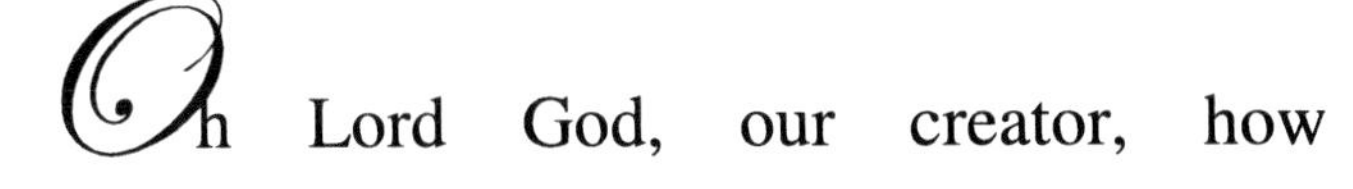

Oh Lord God, our creator, how wonderful is your creation.

You looked out on nothing, empty space, and with your fantastic creative ability You created electrons, neutrons and protons, which You caused to come together to form matter.
From this matter you formed air, water and land.
Then in this water and land you created living creatures,
giving them magnificent forms, amazing anatomical and physiological systems, which enabled
them to
take on nourishment, move about, and
reproduce.
When all was ready, You created your
masterpiece.
You created man and woman.
You made them much more sophisticated
than
your other creatures. You gave them feelings,
and more than that You gave them the ability
to reason.

But even then you were not through. You
placed in
each of them part of yourself in order that

they could know their creator, and love their creator. Knowing this
they might love each other, or if they chose
they could deny their creator, and despise each other.

You knew from the beginning that mankind would find joy and happiness if they would follow your plan. You
also knew that unless mankind learned this plan for
themselves, they would think it would not work. So you
have led man through history to the present, patiently waiting.

You placed mankind in an environment free from anxiety and stress. You gave them plenty to eat and much to enjoy.
They were able to do wonderful things
with the magnificent body you created for them, but they
discovered that part of you in them, and wanted to be God.

They learned they did not have to follow your instructions.
They could go their own way. They rejoiced in their new
found freedom in which they could make their own choices,
and did not have to obey you. The consequences were catastrophic but they

could go their own way.

Then their lives became filled with anxiety and stress
as they struggled for power and possessions which
they equated with being godly. However they could
never accumulate enough to make themselves happy.
So you gave them ten rules with which they
could govern their lives.

You patiently waited while they added to your rules additional
instructions, complicating them beyond reason, and making
them impossible to follow. You watched them struggle to appear
obedient while going their own way. You tolerated evil and
disobedience in generation after generation.

In your time you activated your plan to come into the world
in the form of Jesus, to show us in person how we could
live abundantly being faithful to the spirit of the law.
Jesus was a sensation! He gathered a large following, stirred
up the establishment, and created a great deal of excitement.

But when He failed to take on the role of a warrior king,
his followers, even his closest friends scattered like
a covey of quail. When He was arrested even mighty Peter would not be identified with Him, although
he did stay around
in the crowd to see what happened. Jesus was really not understood before the resurrection, but after He appeared to the twelve, they finally got their act
together, and started spreading the word. However power struggles
and the evil built in us has prevented the Church, yesterday and today from establishing your kingdom as you designed it.

Fortunately, you had another plan. Jesus tried to tell us about this in His parables, but who of us could forgive a child who
demanded his inheritance, then proceed to blow it away on
irresponsible living, only to come crawling back when he found
he couldn't support himself. Only you have that much love.

Only you, Lord, have the love to give each of us equally,
regardless of our behavior, life style, or disposition in the past.

If we will only turn to you, ask to be forgiven, seek to mend
our ways and try to establish a relationship with you, You stand there with open arms waiting for us to come and see.

Your love is more than we can comprehend. You gave us this
wonderful life, this magnificent earth, sky, and outer space, plus
the intelligence to live here and be creative. You gave us the law
to show us how we could live in the Kingdom here on earth. You
knew from the beginning that we would need more.

You gave us Jesus, and then after we killed Him, you raised Him up
to demonstrate what you could do. Then you gave us the Holy Spirit for our comforter and teacher. You have promised to be
always present when we need you. When ever we are ready
You are ready for us.

Oh Lord my God, how can you love us so much? What keeps us
from accepting your love? Why do we insist on "doing it my way"?
Why don't we recognize that this unending supply of love you
have for us can be shared with others, even

those we cannot
Love. Oh Lord my God, have mercy on us.

Amen

Psalm 2

I was sitting quietly in the brush,

hopeful that I might see
one of your greatest creations, a white tail deer, when
out of the corner of my eye I saw some movement
in the grass.
I did not move.
Out of the grass emerged
a tiny cottontail rabbit, not five inches long.
He was not afraid.
He sniffed and nibbled toward me, on he came, sniffing
and nibbling.
I did not move.
He came right up to my boot, sniffed and moved on,
disappearing into the brush. He never knew I was there.
What a wonderful experience for me, Lord. What a
magnificent creation you have caused to be.
Thank you Lord God for your great gift of
life and the ability to enjoy it. Thank you
Lord for all of your Creation. I know you love
us beyond understanding
because you have done so much for us.
Lord God, our creator, I praise your Holy

name.

Amen

Amen

Amen

Psalm 3

Oh my God, where are you when I

need you?
I cry out for you and I hear no answer.
I look around and see you in all your creation,
but I don't feel the comfort of your presence.
Why do you abandon me this way?
Did you not hear me calling out to you?
I need you desperately.
Things were going so good. I was doing so well.
Every one reached out to me, and praised me.
I was lifted up in spirit with their acceptance and praise.
Then I was left alone, abandoned by my friends.
I was alone.
Then when I looked for you, you were gone.
You have always been there, and you promised
to be there when I needed you. What has happened?
Did I leave you, Lord? Did I get so wrapped up in myself
that I left your presence? Why would I do this?
You are my strength and my security.
You give my life meaning. Without you I am nothing.

It is that part of you that is in me that gives me worth.
Hold on to me, Lord. Don't let me go astray.
To be alone is too painful. I need you Lord.
Hold me close to you.
Thank you, Lord.

Amen

Psalm 4

Lord my God and creator, I am troubled.
My wife of over fifty years and I have lived all these years in a loving relationship.
We have enjoyed the warmth and joy you promised.
And we have respected each other and rejoiced in our love of you.
We have not been unfaithful to our marriage vows,
and we have not looked outside our union
for comfort and solace, except to you.
Many of those you love no longer accept your way.
It has become acceptable to ignore the vows we make,
and feel it unnecessary to make any commitment at all.
This is not how you had it planned, this in not part of your plan.
Help us Lord, have mercy on us, and forgive us. Open our eyes to your love and grace. Lord have mercy.

Amen

Psalm 5

Oh Lord my God, giver of every perfect gift,
stay by our side as we struggle through another Lent.
That time every year when we relive the events
leading up to the passion and crucifixion of our Lord Jesus.
Once again we are reminded of our fragile faith
and our intolerance for your unlimited goodness.
We find it impossible to stay close to your immeasurable love for us.
We are compelled to either run away from it,
or attempt to kill it.
That is what we did to our Lord Jesus. We killed Him.
But you didn't let us get away with it, did you?
You raised Him from the dead, and gave Him back to us.
Not only that, He promised to never leave us again.
He will be with us always. You would think we would get the message,
wouldn't you?

Why are we still running? Why is it so hard to let you love us?
Why do we continue to insist on doing it our way?
Every time we choose our way in place of your way, we choose to repeat the crucifixion.
You must be getting tired of it Lord.
Thank you God for your patience, we need all the help we can get.
Lord have mercy on us.

Amen

Psalm 6

Come Lord Jesus, friend and savior,

fill the void that separates us.
Come Lord Jesus, advocate and companion
let me know you hear my prayer.
Send the Holy Spirit to comfort me,
and make my life whole.
My life is lacking and empty when
I don't feel your presence.
My possessions, prestige, and power
cannot replace your presence.
No amount of praise and glory can
replace your love.
Praise and glory feel good for awhile but
soon the feeling is gone.
Come Lord Jesus, friend and savior,
fill my life again.

Amen

Psalm 7

Lord my God of all creation, what a wonder you are.
I know you hear my prayers and those of all who pray,
because the prayers are all answered.
Sometimes you say "yes", sometimes you say "no",
and sometimes you say "not yet".
I know at times as I pray, reciting prayers from memory,
or reading prayers from Holy Scripture or a book,
my mind races through the events of the day,
feeling good about what I have done right,
and making excuses for those things I have done wrong.
I wonder how you feel when you hear this cacophony of scrambled thoughts and words of praise.
Do you have a super filter, which eliminates the trash?
I think not. I think you hear it all.
I think the words of praise and thanksgiving
provide a beautiful background of sweet music
to accompany the thoughts that fill my mind.

You come to know me as only You can, and You are in a position to answer my prayers with
the answer, which is best for me.
Lord my God of all creation, what a wonder you are.

Amen Amen Amen Amen

Psalm 8

Oh Lord God, my creator and source of

life,
I praise Your name for your creative ability.
We have talked before about how wonderful
is this body You have given us.
Only a loving artist such as you are
could have accomplished what you have.
You have given us all we need to do the work
You have planned for us to do, even
providing
us with the need to rest and sleep to repair
the damage we incur from our bad habits
and useful work.
However it has occurred to me, and please
forgive me
for suggesting an improvement, that we waste
a great deal of time sleeping. Six to eight
hours
a day are spent in absolute unproductive
sleep.
If you had created us in such a way that we
didn't
require sleep, just think of all the things we
could get done.
We could stay awake during a dull sermon;
we could
not doze off while reading Holy Scripture; we
could feed

the hungry, clothe the naked, and visit the lonely, if
we didn't have to sleep.
Now that I have suggested this, why does it sound
like a bad idea?
You know that if we had more time we would not use it any more creatively than the time you have given us.
Thank you Lord for being so patient with us.
We need all the help we can get.
Guide and direct us to do those things which will glorify You and establish your kingdom soon.

Amen

Psalm 9

Lord God Almighty your generosity and love are beyond our belief and understanding.
Your planning and structure of all creation has been done in such a way that all of the problems have been anticipated and solved in your mind before you acted, and you accomplished the task by just speaking the words "Let it be."
Your words are all powerful, but our words are powerful too. A word of gratitude to friend or stranger has the power to change the entire day for someone. A word of encouragement gives power and strength to a tired labourer.
A kind word to a lover can build a greater relationship, and a joyous word to anyone can spread that joy.
On the other hand, an unkind word can be as destructive as a slap in the face.
An untrue word can start an avalanche of devastation which can destroy a person or a relationship.
Our words have the power to be creative or destructive.
Lord God help us use our power to glorify you.
We know too well how to glorify ourselves.

Amen

Psalm10

Lord God of all creation, I have a problem.

I have known you for a long, long time. I have felt your presence daily as we visit at prayer.
I have seen the results or your mighty creative hand
in all you have done for us, yet at times I feel I don't
know you at all. I am confused. I don't understand
why tragic things happen to those you love? Why
do we kill each other, why do we steal, lie, and malign
our fellow human beings? Could it be that you do not
exist? Could it be that we have made you up to help
us tolerate the selfishness of mankind and to give us
hope in a hopeless situation? I think not. I think you
are real and your love for us is real. I think you want
us to trust you and to study about you all our lives.
I also think we will not know all about you in this life,

but by constantly searching for you we will stay close to you.
That is all I pray for, Lord, to stay close to you. You
will provide me with all my needs, protect me from my
enemies, and instruct me in your will.
Thank you Lord God for your love.

Amen

Psalm 11

Lord God, Eternal God, magnificent

provider of
all creation, I think you have a problem. There are
more and more of those you love who don't love you.
Even though you have provided us with a wonderful body and
with everything we need to live creative and fruitful
lives, we are not satisfied.
We want more and more. We pray for things we don't
need and make promises we know we will not keep.
We try to bargain with you when we should surrender
to you and allow you to use us in your master plan.
True, there are some of us who practice the art of
worship in your behalf, but most of us fail in responding
appropriately to your great gift of love. We shudder in fear
that we will not have enough to survive. We estimate our

worth and that of our neighbors by the things we accumulate.
We fail to trust your promise that if we believe in you,
we will have life abundantly. We want to be in charge
just in case you don't really know what we need.
I pray that you knew this would happen, and still trust
us to eventually know you better, trust you more, and
return the love you have for us in a way that will let
you know that your plan is working. We must have
Your help Lord.

Amen *Amen* *Amen*

Gracious Lord God of all gifts, one of your greatest gifts is your gift of grandchildren.

Like no other relationship, our love of grandchildren provides joy and happiness that is unbelievable. No pride satisfies like the pride of being the one who is selected to "Come play with me."

Or to stand in awe as one of our little ones takes their place in the All Star line up.

Or to swell with pride as another occupies a chair in the All City Orchestra. What a gift. Knowing that we are not responsible for their manners or other of life's important teachings makes our relationship even more precious. We can enjoy loving them, and watching them grow and develop into wonderful creatures of your magnificent universe.

This must be how You look at all of your creatures, seeing them as what and who they might become, not seeing their faults and forgiving their attempts to escape your loving care. You wait patiently for their return, always being available to guide them back to you. What a wonderful thing you have done for us, allowing us to be grandparents and loving a few of your creatures as you love us.

Psalm 13

Oh Lord our God, Creator and Sustainer,

we are in trouble. I am distraught about the behavior of those you love. For years after the last time we tried to destroy each other in a world wide war, we seemed to be doing better. Even non-believers recognized that the rules you gave us to live by made life better. Our numbers grew, we built more houses of worship and we were at peace.

Recently we have changed. At one time every one accepted that honesty, fidelity, and dependability were ideal attributes of conduct. That is no longer true.

Now many of those You love feel that adultery, promiscuity, and dishonesty are not only acceptable but are the preferred attributes of behavior. Moreover they do not preclude one's election to high office.

You must be very discouraged too. You gave us rules to live by in order that we could enjoy your Kingdom now.

When that didn't work you sent Jesus to show us how you planned for us to live. He got too close to us and we killed Him. You forgave us for that and raised Him from the dead, and sent us the

Holy Spirit to comfort and teach us. You will not give up on us, will You? How can You love us that much?
You must see us, not as we are, but as we could be.
You patiently wait for us to see Your way. You rejoice when we turn toward you. You would like for us to see that wonderful potential in each other, and rejoice with You. When that time comes, all the Company of Heaven will rejoice.
O Lord my God, how great You are.

Amen Amen Amen Amen

Psalm 14

Lord God of all wisdom and knowledge,

today I had a message, which must have been from You.
A sign on a local church announced that "Prayer is a Declaration of Dependence."
How true that is, and what a wonderful answer
to the popular song which declares and brags that " I'll do it my way."
I have known for years that my natural tendency is to want to do it my way, but when I listened to that song I knew that something was missing.
I have tried rewriting the lyrics changing
"My Way" to "God's Way" but it has never worked out.
Now I have the theme I need, now I can sing and
shout my Declaration of Dependence on You.
You know and I know that I will fail at times, and I will still do it my way, but that is not my wish, but my sinful nature directing me.

My prayer is that most of the time I will take my direction from my dependence on You.
Lord God of all wisdom and Knowledge,
how great You are.

Amen

Amen

Amen

Amen

Psalm 15

h Lord, our creator and master programmer,
what a wonderful body and mind you have given us.
I have praised You before for Your fine work,
and it causes me to shudder with fear when I
suggest that you might have done better, but
I have discovered a minor adjustment you could
make which would make our life much better.
As you well know, we often let our more ungracious
self act in such a way that others are injured.
We almost always recognize this malicious action
for what it is immediately, and wish it undone.
When I make an error on my computer, I can
press two keys, and the error will be undone.
Now would that not be a handy tool for correcting
our errors in behavior? I know we have the
ability to tell you what we have done, and be
forgiven, but even if we apologize to the injured one,
he is still injured. It would be so much better if
one could just zap the deed undone.

Being one
of yours is not easy Lord, but it is so comforting.
Thank You Lord God for Your love.

Amen

Psalm 16

Oh Lord my God and creator, how you

must suffer
over your creation daily. Only today one of those you
love has destroyed himself. True he had wandered far from the path you set for us, but I know your heart must be broken over his action. Surely he knew of your love from his parents. He must have known acceptance and approval as a baby when his proud father held him in his loving arms. Maybe not.
As he grew, surely he must have known you through
others who knew and loved you, and told him of you.
Maybe not. Do you suppose he lived out his evil life
and was never introduced to you? No wonder he despaired and destroyed himself. I think we who know and love you are responsible for his life and death. Lord have mercy on us, sinners that we are.

Amen

Amen

Amen

Psalm 17

Lord God our creator, what a wonderful

God you are.
You have given us many wonderful gifts, but as I was
having lunch today I realized what a magnificent thing
You did when you caused us to pause three times daily
and take on nourishment. You could have designed us
in such a way that our nourishment could have been
provided by photosynthesis, like the plants, but you, in
all your wisdom, provided a mechanism by which we
could enjoy the fruits of your Kingdom three times daily,
while restoring the fuel on which we operate. Not only that,
you created an unending variety of luscious foods that
not only supply our fuel needs, but are delightful to the taste.
It's no wonder that when I sit down to eat, the first thing
I think
is "Thank You Lord".

I know there are some of those you love that do not have enough
to eat. It is not because you have not provided it. It is because
some of us are not concerned about them, and some of us
are too greedy and want more than our share. Many of us abuse the wonderful body you have given us
by eating more than we need, but it does taste so good. And
to some of us the food supplies the love and acceptance we
don't find in our community. This too is not your fault Lord, it
is ours. Have mercy on us, Lord; we are trying to learn your way.
Thank you Lord for your great gift of life, and all that goes with it.

Psalm 18

Lord God of hope and mercy, how wonderful You are.
You have anticipated all of our needs, and have supplied
them before we knew we wanted them. You have answered
all of our problems before we knew we had a problem.
When we recognize our problem, we set out to solve it
without talking to you. We think we know what we need,
because the world tells us what will make us happy.
How mistaken we are. The evil in us tempts us with
money and power, when what we need is your counsel.
We need to remember the relationship we have with you.
You have created an environment in which you have
known what our problems would be, and have provided
solutions before we encounter the problem. We are
looking for a life free of problems, and think that if we

accumulate enough wealth and material things we will
have that life. Some of us never know that you have
created that state for us. All we need do is walk with
Your Holy Spirit daily, and He will direct us.
Lord God of hope and mercy, thank you for all Your
many gifts of love. How great You are.

Amen

Psalm 19

Lord our God and Creator, architect of

our magnificent body, how great you are.
I never cease to wonder at the beauty and versatility of the structure You have given us to live in while we are earth bound.
My body has served me well, with the help of skilled surgeons, physicians, and prayer in spite of my indiscretions and abuse.
However, and again I shudder when I say this,
I can think of a small modification you might make if you ever make another model.
I have noted that some of the parts are stronger than others, and last longer.
Some of the most important parts wear out before others, leaving us still alive but unable to function as well as we were designed to function.
It is true many of us make remarkable adjustments to this kind of loss, but it might be better if all our parts wore out at the same time.
I understand that our abuse and misuse of our body is probably responsible for many of these failures, but this is not always true.
I also understand that our ability to function in spite of malfunction of some vital part demonstrates the resilience of this great body

You have given us, although it never works quite as good as the original model.
There is a great deal that I don't understand and I am certain that You have a good reason for making us as we are, so please forgive me for trying to improve on Your design. I have spent many years trying to help some of those You love adjust to malfunctioning body parts, and I have suffered with them. I have also rejoiced with them when they make a satisfactory recovery with medical skills
and prayer. Maybe this is the way you planned it and You had a hand in their recovery and rehabilitation.
Oh Lord my God, how great you are.

Amen

Amen

Amen

Amen

Psalm 20

Lord God of all creation, what a wonderful gift

you have given us in the ability to laugh. It was a loving touch that only you could have created.
You knew we would need the healing, tranquillizing effect of a good hearty laugh to help us through some
of the hard times we will face. You knew that at times we
would need something to break the destructive tension
which was about to destroy a relationship, and you equipped us with a sense of humor to replace that tension with laughter. What a wonderful gift.
It is true that at times we use this gift in a harmful way to belittle some of those you love. We take pleasure in making others the subject of our humor forgetting how painful it is to them. It makes us feel good to make people laugh, even at the expense of others.
Is this that evil force that dwells deep within us? The force
that causes us to misuse many of your wonderful gifts?
Lord God of goodness and grace, I pray you drive this
evil force away and stay close to us to prevent its return.

Amen

Psalm 21

Oh Lord my God, creator of everything there

is, You have done it again.
Here in the middle of winter, when we should be under dark clouds, shivering in the cold,
You have given us this beautiful day.
The sky is clear and blue, there is not
a dark cloud anywhere. There are a few
white puffy clouds which contrast in grandeur against the gorgeous blue sky.
The temperature is crisp and cool, and
there is a gentle breeze blowing.
The songbirds are singing as if it were spring.
It causes the earth to shout with joy,
and reminds those you love that we haven't
been abandoned. We rejoice and sing with the songbirds. What a wonderful God you are.
We thank you for your gifts of love, and praise
Your holy name as we wonder about your power.

Amen

Amen

Amen

Psalm 22

Gracious Lord of all time, how wise you are.

Your knowledge of Your creation is timeless, and what was true in the beginning will be true forever.

Your law that you gave us years ago is as true today as it was ages ago when you first revealed it.

Israel loved it then and now, as does your new Israel,

but there is a problem. We have learned of your love from Your Son Jesus, and it is much easier to depend on your love, than live by the Law.

We can surrender to any or all of the temptations knowing that when we come back to you, you will forgive us again and again. We know that this will not work unless repentance is on our heart.

You must have known from the beginning that we would be this way. You wrote the Law for our benefit and you knew that if we followed the Law we would stay close to you and experience the abundant life you have planned for us. You also knew that we wouldn't follow the Law, and would need a way of safe return to you,

So You sent us Jesus, to show us how much you
love us. How great you are! Thank you Lord God
for your love for us. We couldn't live without it.

Amen *Amen* *Amen*

Amen

Psalm 23

Lord God our father and creator of all that we

are I have a confession to make. I have said many times before that your design of our body could not be improved upon in structure or function. This has usually come following a complaint about some structure or function, but I have come to realize that You knew
what you were doing when you designed us.
I have just recovered from a respiratory infection, (and I still don't know why you created the virus.), which left me with a cough which terrifies children, and frightens strong men. I prayed to you for relief which you supplied, and I thank you very much, but I wondered at the time why you made the cough.
I know it clears the airway, but it goes on and on long after it is no longer needed. A small drop of clear mucus can hang up just above the larynx and cause havoc with one's social life. Friends and family members run for cover and avoid the cougher at all costs.
It really makes one feel alone and insecure. It is good that you stay at our side, otherwise we would really be alone. I suppose if there were any other way to insure a clear airway you would know about it, but if you ever decide to redesign our wonderful body please

work on a better way to remove foreign bodies from the trachea. We would be pleased to be able to do without the cough.

Amen

Psalm 24

Heavenly Father and provider of all things we need,
thank you for your gift of Holy Scripture.
Of all your wonderful gifts, Holy Scripture stands out as our best picture of who and what you are.
As I read about people and their relationship with you I find that no one comes into your presence without being aware of your greatness and magnificence, and it often makes them uncomfortable and uneasy.
One cannot be near You without knowing how great You are and how little and insignificant we are.
And yet you love us and continue to bless us with your grace and loving care. What a wonderful God You are. How can we respond to a love like yours? Is all you require a returned love and a declaration of that love in our worship and witness to those who don't know you? It doesn't seem like much for all You have done for us, yet you continue to love and forgive us, and wait for us with your loving arms open and ready to hold us close to You.
My how great you are. Thank you for your love.

Amen *Amen* *Amen*

Psalm 25

Oh Lord our God and creator, how wonderful and perceptive you are. You knew that there would be times when, in our attempt to drive our own lives, we would fall into depression and despair. You knew we would stray from your influence and grace, thinking our affluence and position were sufficient to sustain us. You knew that we would try to be in charge of our being. You also knew that we would fail and fall from our high esteem of ourselves, causing a feeling of frustration and depression.

Knowing this would happen to us, you not only provided a method of rescue from this destructive mood, but you created a way we might avoid falling again.

Our escape comes from gathering with others of those you love to hear your story again, and to feel Your presence in our lives. We can avoid this desperate situation by staying close to Your faithful ones, and developing a positive attitude by knowing and feeling your love for us at all times.

You really are alive in us. What a spectacular way to distribute your love and grace. You are indeed a magnificent God. Thank You. *Amen*

Psalm 26

God our father and creator, how perceptive you are. You know us much better than we know ourselves. You have provided us with untold riches, and have given us the talent and ability to take them for our own, knowing that our possession of them will tend to negate our need for you. We perceive that in their possession we can demonstrate our worth. We feel indestructible, not subject to any disease, disorder, or failure. The Dow-Jones average is the barometer of our value, and it can only go up.

We forget that the thing that makes us worthy is your love for us. But You haven't left us without help. You know that all the possessions and prestige the world can offer is never enough, and you have provided a way for us to find our way back to you. You know that when this worldly life fails us, we will suffer. Then we will remember from whence comes our worth.

What a wonderful, loving, patient father You are.

Thank you, father, for your love.

Amen

Psalm 27

Lord God of all wisdom and knowledge,

what a wonderful gift you have given us,
the gift of our awareness of our mortality.
It is true that most of our life we are in denial about it, but from time to time we are reminded of the truth that our life on earth is limited. When we take hold of this concept solidly, we really begin to live. We begin to live if we are close to you. When we know you, and know how much you love us, we are able to turn loose of the fear of death that keeps us from being the person you expect us to be. We are able to love our neighbour
and the stranger in our midst, as well as love ourselves. We can grow closer to you and accept the fact that you have a plan for us
to be with you. Then we will
understand all of those mysteries that confuse us now. Thank you, Lord God,
for your love for us and for sharing your magnificent creation with us.

Amen

Psalm 28

Lord God Almighty our creator,

whose existence
makes possible our hope, what a wonderful gift is that hope. The hope that your presence gives us is the hope that makes for the good life we all yearn for and seek. Sometimes we fail to recognize that you are the author of that hope and look to luck or destiny in which to hope for access to the good life. We don't see that our hope in you is what makes for the good life. And the good life is the consequence of our hope in you. Thank you Lord God for the hope You give us. Life is impossible without it.

Amen

Amen

Amen

Psalm 29

Thank you Lord God for the Holy Scriptures and thank you for preachers who teach from them week after week. I learn more about you and your love for us from these Holy Scriptures and the dedicated people who make us aware of all that you have given us, and what you still have in store for us. From the parable of the landowner who let his vineyard out to the greedy tenants we were taught that you are the landowner of our lives, and we are the tenants. Our life's job is to take care of the life you have given
us, and be productive for you. Not only that, You have not gone off into a far land, rather You are right beside us all the time to empower us to do your work and be creative for you.

All too often we are greedy like those in the parable, and abuse the life you have entrusted to us. Too frequently we take credit for the success we have, forgetting that all we have to work with is what you have given us, and all we accumulate is already yours. We behave
as if our praiseworthy existence is due to our own shrewdness and ability and not a gift from you.

It must sadden you mightily for us, the heirs of all that You have created, to behave in such a despicable manner. Yet you love us, and forgive us as if we were behaving in the way you designed us to live, at our
greatest potential. What a wonderful landowner You are, God, and what a pleasure it is to know you are right beside us to care for us and help us work for you.

Amen

Amen

Amen

Psalm 30

Lord God of all creation, may your name be praised forever. Not only have you created an environment for us that is delightful and wonderful, but you have given us a handbook of instructions to teach us how to reap the maximum pleasure in it. The Holy Scriptures instruct us in such a way that our lives can be productive, creative, enjoyable and a credit to you, if we will but follow the directives. The instruction comes from hearing the Word preached, from our own reading, and from many unexpected sources. On the day we memorialize the trial and crucifixion of our Lord Jesus Christ, we read the story of that terrifying day from the Gospel, and at the point in the story when our Lord gives up his life, we always pause, and stand in silence to meditate on the significance of the moment.

One day, at this point, the silence was broken by the shout of a child who asked,

"WHAT HAPPENED?"

What happened indeed? We murdered our Lord and Savior. Before He died, He prayed that we should be forgiven. Forgiven then and forgiven now. How can we ever thank you enough? How can we ever repay that wonderful act of mercy? Only by accepting your gift of Grace, which you give freely and lovingly to your Creation because you love us more than we can understand. How great you are, oh Lord our God.

Amen

Amen

Amen

Amen

Psalm 31

Lord God our creator, Lord Jesus our advocate and Savior, Lord Holy Spirit, our comforter and teacher, what a wonderful thing you have done for us in giving us life. Not only have you created us, but you have given us this extraordinary world to live in. You have given us intelligence, feelings, and the ability to know right from wrong. You have also given us a set of directions which, if we follow them, will insure that we will live fruitful, creative, productive lives that will please you.

The trouble is your expectations of us are impossible to fulfill. There is no way we can love some of the people that you love. They treat us badly, rob us and drag us into court and defame us. They murder people, do unthinkable things to children, beat their wives, ignore and dishonor their parents, and yet you love them. How can you love them? You must see them as they would be if they behaved as you planned. You must know their potential and see and love them, as they might be if they knew you.

How can we see them, as you know them? Where do we get the patience and tolerance that you have? If you love them as they are who don't know you, will you love us who know you, even when we fall short of your expectations?

That is good news, if it is true, and I believe it is. That is what Jesus is trying to teach us. While your expectations are impossible, your patience is never ending, your love for us immeasurable and your power is greater than all the evil in creation.

ALLELUIA!

Amen

Amen

Amen

Amen

Psalm 32

Lord God of all intelligence, I know you are rejoicing today. You must have had a hearty laugh, and shouted,

"AT LAST."

How long have you waited for the scientific community to recognize that what you have been telling us for eons can be documented as factual and true. It has been scientifically established that being loved by someone and loving someone is healthier than being alone.

Eureka. Now we know that people who are depressed, lonely and isolated are much more likely to suffer a serious illness, even die, than those who live in a loving community. It is also said that diet, healthy lifestyle, genetics, drugs or surgery, or any miracles of modern medicine don't have as much effect on health as living in a warm loving relationship. You, dear Lord, have been telling us that we could have the abundant life if we would follow your way. Does it bother you that we must have the authentication of the medical community before we will accept this gift from you?

I think not. I believe that you are behind this "discovery", and are celebrating with all the company of heaven it's publication.

Thank you, Lord our God, You are a wonder.

Amen

Amen

Amen

Amen

Psalm 33

Lord God our governor and creator, this has been a wonderful week for you, and all believers. Not only has the medical community recognized that one is healthier and will live longer if one lives in a loving relationship, but now the psychological community has acknowledged that in spite of a booming economy and a runaway stock market, the incidence of despair and depression is pandemic. Could it be that what you have taught us from the beginning is true? Is it a fact that material possessions will not bring us peace and the good life described by the Madison Ave. crowd?
How can this be? Billions have been spent molding our taste and desires, and our expectations. How can they be wrong? Surely it is wealth that will save us. We have learned this from birth. We shall embrace it and not be afraid. For gold is our stronghold, and sure defense, and it will be our savior. How can we draw near with rejoicing hearing these frightening words? The pleasure of riches has been made known among the people, and has been exalted forever. Praises have been sung and are known throughout the world. Must we now cry out in despair and forsake our joy in worldly goods?

Where can we go for solace, where can we find peace?

At last we have asked the right question. You are the answer, Lord. You have told us this from the beginning of time. How patient can you be?
How long will you love us? Thank you Lord God,
Have mercy on us.

Amen

Psalm 34

Lord God of all that is, I am frightened.

I was awakened by the most horrible nightmare I have ever experienced, and I am aghast. In my dream I entered a great cathedral and noted there was a worship service in progress. The altar was covered with a gold lame, and the Cross had been replaced with a large dollar sign, and above it was a constant report of the stock market changes. The nave was filled with worshipers who were singing. The music was familiar, but I had never heard the lyrics before. I shall never forget them, they were so terrifying.

"*Surely it is cash which saves me,*
I will trust in it and not be afraid.
The bank is my stronghold and my sure defense,
and it will be my savior.
from there I will draw gold with rejoicing,
from a source that never fails.
And on each day I will say
give thanks to the bank and kneel down
to it's name.
I know I can walk among the people,
knowing full well that my name is exalted,

I know they will sing my praises for I have
done great things and my wealth is ever growing.
Bow down ye servants of Mammon, and sing out with joy
for the greed that is in you is the nature of man, and so
it shall be for ever."

Assure me Lord that this will never come to pass. I know You have promised that you have overcome the world, and I believe that you have, but there is a force still abroad that is trying to take it back. Lord deliver me from any more dreams such as this. Thank you, Lord, I praise your name.

Amen

Psalm 35

Lord God our creator, what a magnificent Father you are. At worship this day we prayed "O God, who wonderfully created, and yet more wonderfully restored, the dignity of human nature," and I was reminded again what a blessing You have bestowed on us to be created in your image.

And again I was made aware of your generosity in that You constantly restore that dignity when we fail to demonstrate it in our lives. We constantly fall short of the people you created us to be. We abuse the glorious body you have given us.

We seek pleasure and security in attaining power and wealth rather than finding satisfaction in your promise of the abundant life in your Kingdom. You must love us very much to continue to save us from ourselves as you do.

I pray that you will persist in your love, because it feels so good to return to your loving arms and protection after we have gone astray. Do not give up on us Lord.

Amen

Psalm 36

Lord God of creation and giver of the law of life, I am troubled. In reading Holy Scripture I find your servant, Paul, telling the Church in Rome
that if they didn't obey your law they would burn in hell. Yet all I know about You tells me that You do not want us to burn in hell. You want us for your own. My expectation from reading Holy Scripture is that You are a loving, forgiving God, and the last thing You want is to see us burn in hell. I am sure Paul knew what he was talking about,
but he doesn't cut us any slack. No one knows us better than You, Lord, and You know our weakness and how we are going to be in and out of a sinful activity all the time.
We come to You in prayer and ask to be forgiven, and our Priest says we are forgiven. We say that we repent, and then go out and sin again. You must get very discouraged with us, and feel like letting us destroy Your creation.
I wouldn't blame You if You did, but please Lord be patient with us. I see a few signs of our improvement. Recently I have learned that medical doctors have acknowledged that
prayer will help healing. Now that is a step in the right direction. There is hope for us, only if you will stay close to us and open our hearts to your Holy

Spirit. Stay with us, Lord, Your mercy is great and we can't live without it.

Amen Amen Amen Amen

Psalm 37

My God and Father, my creator, how great You are.
My God and Holy Spirit, You are wonderful.
My God and savior, Jesus, what a gift You have given us.
Yesterday as I lay alone in the CT scanner
awaiting its probing analysis of my tumor, I
sought You out for comfort. I was not disappointed.
I asked, "Why did You create malignant cells?"
You provided the answer without hesitation.
"When I created you, I built into you the freedom of choice. You are free to follow my design, or go your own way. You are made up of individual living cells which also possess the freedom of choice. Just like you they sometime disobey their creator, and go their own way. They were given a plan to follow, but they choose to go their own way and become malignant. Sometime their fellow cells suppress and destroy them. At times they repent and revert to the way they were created.
At times they overcome the host organism and destroy it.
But just as I love you as you are, I love them as they are, and pray that they will repent and return to the way I made them.
Nothing I have made is unworthy of my love."
I thank You for this revelation, my Lord and Creator. It makes me more comfortable. But You

need to know that I can't love them as You do, and I will be praying with You that they will repent. Moreover I hope to send that part of me on to You ahead of me with the help of my friendly surgeon. I'll be along when You call me, but if it be your will, I will stay here a bit longer. I do enjoy this life You have given me and I thank You for it.

Amen Amen Amen Amen

Psalm 38

Lord of my life, where did You go? You have always been near when I needed You. Why have You deserted me? In my pain and insecurity I looked for You, I sought Your help, but You were gone, and I was alone.
I cried out but heard no answer. I was sinking deeper into the pit of despair, and felt abandoned.
Then You came to me from Holy Scripture in a vision of Peter asking you for help to walk on water. He did well as long as he kept his eyes on You, but when he thought about himself, he started sinking, sinking like I was. Then I knew where You had gone.
I had taken my eyes off you, and left You. You did not leave me. My spirits brightened, I was no longer in pain nor fearful, I was healing again. Thank You, Lord.
Thank You for Your constant presence and perpetual help. I know I will heal if I stay close to You. You are my strength and my salvation and always will be.
Thank You Lord.

Amen *Amen* *Amen*

Psalm 39

Lord God of heaven and earth, what a magnificent thing You have done when you designed and created our body.
Of all the wonderful features, the ability to self heal is the greatest. I have seen bone, seemingly shattered beyond repair, unite into solid bone if placed and kept in alignment for a spell. I have seen muscle and tendon, ripped asunder, repair itself. Recently I have had the occasion to experience personally one of your greatest miracles. A section of my intestine was removed, then the cut ends were placed and secured to each other.
Now that organ is functioning again as it was designed, completely healed, and good as new. What a wonder You are. Thank You Lord for this glorious body and its
ability to heal itself. The life You have given me is fantastic and I enjoy it every day, and I do appreciate the body you have provided me. Perhaps I could do a better job of caring for it, if I will keep it in mind. What an awesome gift it is. Thank You, Father.

Psalm 40

Lord God, our creator and provider of life, and all that it takes to enjoy it abundantly,
What an awesome wonder You are.
From the beginning of creation, You have given us all we need, and You have made it possible for us to refuse Your gifts. You have given us freedom of choice. We can accept Your gifts, follow Your instructions, and be happy, or we can accept Your gifts and do our own thing, and fight the world alone. We can go our own way, and You still love us. You have given us many laws and instructions, but all You have really asked us is to trust You. Trust You when we need help that You will be there. Trust You when the world seems to come down on us. Trust You when we are sick unto death and suffering with depression, thinking about the end of life, as we know it. "Just trust me,"You say and I hear You. You are an awesome wonder. Thank You Father for Your gift of life everlasting.

Amen *Amen* *Amen*

Psalm 41

Lord God of all intelligence and source of all knowledge,
what a wonderful gift you have given us in the life and teachings of our Lord Jesus. We can know Him through Holy Gospel and the letters of the Apostles.
We have learned about the extravagant love you have for us from His life and His demonstration of how you expect us to live our lives. He showed us the way to live together in peace and tranquility, how to love the unlovable, and how to be a peacemaker in the face of hostility. He taught us many things, but probably the most important is that we should love one another, and not try to straighten each other out.

Thank you Father, you are fantastic.

Amen

Psalm 42

Lord God my creator, I am troubled.

What has happened
to my enthusiasm, my vim and vigor, my joy of being alive? I drag my feet when I walk, I move as if in slow motion. Ideas don't excite me and I am constantly fatigued. I could take to my bed and retreat from this life.
Why is this happening to me? I know you love me. My creator, the creator of the universe and all there is loves me, what more do I need? You have promised to stand beside me and comfort me. Why do I ignore this love and comfort? You have given me a wonderful body to live in.
True, I have abused it. I have fouled my coronary arteries, and developed a malignancy, but you have wonderful healing power, which will free me from these maladies.
Yet I struggle with my lack of control. I want to be in charge.
Are you trying to tell me something, my Lord? Am I trying to take your place? Must I learn this over and over again?
Why did you make me so fragile, so forgetful, and so determined to be in charge? When I don't trust you I get in trouble, Please increase my faith and trust, Lord.

You are my strength and salvation. Come to me with your love and comfort me, I am a disaster without you.

Amen Amen Amen Amen

Psalm 43

My Lord and Creator, I have learned something today.
On our television this morning I saw a handsome, athletic woman, dancing with joy and exclaiming "I feel good!"
I would have thought that she had won a large cash prize, or a trip around the world, she was so happy. I wondered what could give her that glorious feeling, and I knew that she had just heard about your love for us. That is the way I feel when I consider the gift of your grace. As I continued to listen I learned that her ecstasy did not come from a religious experience, nor did she win a magnificent prize.
She was overjoyed because the laxative she took last night had worked. If she does not know you, I would love to be around when she meets you. There will be a fabulous Celebration. She probably does not really know what joy is.

Amen Amen Amen Amen

Psalm 44

Lord God our Heavenly Father and creator, what a wonderful mystery you have produced. Recently I was in a discussion about "faith in God" and we were trying to define it. After struggling for awhile, our leader stated that faith was a yearning that God does exist, and
not an intellectual understanding of the Apostles' Creed.
What an extraordinary concept, and very helpful. Not all of us can discern the complexity of the theology of the scholars, but we all can hope for your love for us to be true. We know it is more than we deserve, but the idea that our Creator does exist, and is available for and desires our communication and requests, is too good to not believe.
It is not necessary for us to fathom the
depth of the rationale of why you created us to enjoy the fruits of your grace. All we need to do is say "I believe" to you, and we inherit all we will ever need.
The theologians can study, ponder, and explore and maybe understand more, but they will never get any more grace than is available to the believer that says "I believe." You are a wonder, Lord.

Amen *Amen* *Amen*

Psalm 45

Almighty God, I need help. Today I heard a well known Preacher of the Gospel make a remark that I find hard to believe. He said, "All tragic events that we experience are the will of God, and part of His plan."
This doesn't sound like the God I know and love. Am I wrong to disagree?
I think your heart breaks every time our foolish behavior results in a tragedy. I feel you suffer whenever a child dies from any cause. You have a plan for us which inundates us with your love and grace.
While we will encounter tragedies when we break one of your commandments or physical laws, you will always be there to help us work through the pain and suffering. What I know about you from Holy Scripture, your plan for us is to accept your love and grace, and pass it on to everyone we meet.
The life you have given us, with the freedom to choose your way or our way, can be a wonderful adventure, filled with joy and excitement or it can be marred by unhappiness and sorrow. It is our choice. If we fall into a tragic situation we know you will be there to bail us out.
Thank you Lord for the great gift of life and your love.

Amen

Psalm 46

God of all creation, I praise your Holy name.

What a magnificent thing you have done for us. You have given us your love freely for the taking.
You have created an environment in which we can grow and thrive and enjoy the life you have given us. You have given us a plan of life, which will ensure that our life will be joyful, creative, exciting, and challenging. Not only that, the bequest of your love is available to all, regardless of education, intelligence, socio-economic station, or intellectual curiosity.
The fact is you do love us, beyond all reason, as we are, without exception. We can accept it, reject it or ignore it.
What we can't do is deserve it, explain it, or understand it. We can only follow your plan and share it with our fellow creatures. Your love can be appreciated and utilized by any who will accept it in faith without understanding the mystery, yet it will also fascinate and bewilder the scholar who seeks to unravel the mystery. You are a wonder,
O Lord. Thank you for the mystery of life and love.
This life is wonderful.

Amen Amen Amen Amen

Psalm 47

Lord of my life and Heavenly Father, I praise your name.
I have thanked you daily for the life you have given me yet I never seem to thank you enough to express the overwhelming appreciation I feel. How can I tell you how much I look forward to each new day to experience the love you have given us to share with each other?
And particularly that special person you have given me to be my mate, friend, companion, and lover.
The love you have provided us has withstood bleeding peptic ulcers, heart attacks, financial disaster, strokes, and cancer for over 50 years and is still going. I don't believe there is anything life can throw at us that our love cannot withstand. That is the way you planned it, isn't it Lord?
What a magnificent gift you have given us. I pray daily that you will stay close to us so that we will not lose that love divine from you.

Amen *Amen* *Amen*

Psalm 48

Lord God in heaven, I need your help. I am being poisoned, and this magnificent body you have given me is being rendered useless and non-functional. I am listless, lethargic, anorexic, weak, and absent of enthusiasm and the joy of life your presence brings.

I know how Jonah felt in the belly of the whale. I too am lost, and cry out for help. You answered Jonah's cry, please answer mine. Give me the joy of your saving help again. Sustain me with your love and constant presence. You have lifted me out of the depths of depression before, and I know you can do it again. Help me, O Lord my God and Creator; your servant is suffering.

Amen Amen Amen Amen

Psalm 49

My Lord and my God, my Creator and friend, how great you are. What a fantastic thing your friendship is. You are always there to solve what problem we have. And before I say more I want to thank you for the chemicals that are being pumped into my body to fight the Demon that has invaded me. They give me hope to be rid of it, but they make me feel terrible. The chemicals make Me feel like crawling into a deep hole. I have no energy, no ambition, no desire to enjoy the magnificent life you have created for me. They make me sick. Yet because of your love for me I am able to do those things that I need to do in spite of the effects of the chemotherapy. Thank you Lord for giving me the strength and gumption to continue to accomplish the work you have set before me. You are a fabulous God and Savior, and I can't imagine life without you.

Amen

Psalm 50

My Lord and God, what is wrong with me?

My body is not functional because of pain and weakness. I can no longer sleep the night through. I drag myself into the day, the picture of a walking dead man.
The Joy of your presence I no longer feel. I am a wreck. How can I represent your love for mankind in my present depressed state of body and mind?
Yet when I sit here with you I am rejuvenated in mind, and strengthened in body and determination. I am able to muck on with the work you have given me to do. I can only work if you are beside me, giving me your peace and love.
So stay with me my Lord Jesus, and give me your help.

Amen Amen Amen Amen

Psalm 51

Great God of the universe, creator of all that there is, I am puzzled. I have known you for many years, and I feel very close to you. We have talked many times and I regularly renew my pledge to your service. I feel that every one should be aware of our relationship and yet it seems that there is a constant pressure on me to doubt your existence and deny my love for you, and your love for me. I would think that even the Evil One would give up and leave me alone, but even as we talk I feel his presence nearby, trying to be involved in our relationship.

Please, Lord God, surround me with your Guardian Angels to protect me from his evil power, and give me peace.

Only you can save me. Lord have mercy.

Amen Amen Amen

Psalm 52

Lord my God and creator, I have been complaining a great deal recently, and you must be getting put out with me. While I feel your constant presence, it seems to me that as soon as one problem is solved, I am presented with another. Now I do trust you to help me through all of these diseases, but I wonder why, at this advanced age, I should suffer with them. It came to me last night as we were talking, and I was complaining again, that maybe it was being demonstrated to me all of the diseases I have treated during my life as a physician. It lets me see how I have helped those you love,
and painfully points out to me how I have neglected helping some of those you love. Please forgive me for my neglect, and the pride I bathe myself in for those I helped. I thank you each night for *"setting me at tasks which demand my best efforts, and for leading me to accomplishments which satisfy and delight me"*,*but I confess my pride of accomplishment frequently obscures my thanksgiving for you, the real healer.
And now I ask for your healing blessing on me, that I may continue learning your way, and my assignment in your world.

Amen Amen Amen Amen

(*From the 1979 Book of Common Prayer, page 836)

Psalm 53

Lord God, my creator and teacher, I have a problem. At the worship service we read that part of Holy Scripture from Matthew's gospel where you were telling us that when we feed, love, or befriend the least of these, we also feed, love and befriend you. Now this is a wonderful concept, which I endorse wholeheartedly, but it came to me that
You did not mean just the least of these but all of the least of these. Now while my cup is full, it lacks a great deal from running over, and if I gave away everything, I could not feed all of these.
Maybe you are talking about my attitude and not my things. Maybe if I trusted you enough, I would not think about what I am giving away, but rather what I am doing for you. I am not there yet, Lord, but keep working on me,

We have a long way to go.

Amen Amen Amen Amen

Psalm 54

Lord God of my life, I praise your Holy Name. What a wonderful provider and caregiver you are. In my current state of disease and disorder you have been with me at all times. You have comforted me in my pain and despair. You have strengthened me when I have wanted to curse the life you have given me. You have tolerated my lack of faith, and gently reminded me that you have a plan for me, which I have not completed.

I am not sure where you will lead me, but these events which I am experiencing now will prepare me for what is to come. I pray that I will be ready and able to perform in such a way that you will be glorified and given the honor you deserve. All glory be to you, oh Lord my God.

Amen

Amen

Amen

Amen

Psalm 55

Lord God and Father Creator, how wonderful of you to allow the objects of your creation to enjoy the wonders of your conception without even knowing their source. You have made it possible to experience the glory of a sunrise, the beauty in nature, the satisfaction of a fabulous meal without knowing you, their author. You have even permitted your creatures to explore the intricacies of your creation and understand their nature, and even take credit for the discovery, and deny your existence. What a loving, generous, unselfish creator you are. You have made it possible for us to touch, love and know the joy of relationships and not know you as their source. You have given us the power of creation and allowed us to enjoy its triumph and not acknowledge you as the source. Even the most simple forms of life have been given all they need to survive, recreate, and proliferate and not even understand the origin of their power. What a wonder you are. You have even allowed us to design the nature of our close relationships in spite of your explicit instructions.

You permit us to presume that we know what is best for us when we don't even understand your plan for our life. We do not deserve your love and generosity. Thank you Lord.

Amen *Amen* *Amen*

Psalm 56.

Lord God, our creator and benefactor, how great you are. You have created us in such a way that even as an infant we are able to experience the joy and excitement of a loving relationship. A quality of life, a gift from you, that we will have all our life. The gift that makes our life great and wonderful. The gift that makes possible friendships
that enhance and enrich our very existence and brings joy and delight to our daily experience. The gift that makes possible the long term relationships of a couple in marriage, and a family group. What a gift. It is true that we have the option to not respond to the gift. We are free to go our own way and
use people who reach out to us in love and acceptance to our own advantage and ignore the opportunity to return the gift of love to them. You do this because you love us, and have faith in us that we will respond to your love and return to you.
How great you are, how great you are.

Amen *Amen* *Amen*

Psalm 57

My Lord and Creator what a wonderful teacher you are. In my recent troubles I have learned to appreciate your methods and to know anew how responsive You are to my prayers. You know that we are living in an environment of suffering and pain, and have given us a protection and remedy from that disorder. The freedom you have created for us is the same freedom that makes possible the development of the suffering and pain.

We know this, yet we continue to try to direct our own lives without your help, and continue to get in trouble. I have read in Holy Scripture that there is another trouble maker which can cause suffering and pain as well as a false sense of joy and pleasure. This evil force can make us think you have abandoned us or want us to be miserable and unhappy. It is the force that only your power and love can overcome.

We must put on the whole armor of protection that only can come from you, if we but ask. I have asked for and received that protection in my troubles and I rejoice that I know from whence it comes. In my daily prayers I thank you, but I can never thank you enough. Hell must be that condition in which we can no longer know you are near and hear our prayer. Stay close to me, Lord.

Amen. *Amen* *Amen*

Psalm 58

Lord God and Creator of all there is, what a magnificent thing you have given us in a recent reunion of friends. The gathering happened because a large group of those you love experienced a common event sixty years ago: we graduated from the same high school.

Many had kept in touch through the years, and we had met in reunion before, but this seemed to be a special occasion. The one hundred fifty beautiful faces, young, excited, expectant, brave and hungry for what life had in store, had been molded by time, war, sorrow, happiness, achievement, hard work and disease, but were still recognized and a joy to behold. We spent the evening reliving the early days, but mostly we shared the joys and sorrows of the six decades since our graduation. It was a moment in time to review with friends our lives as we had spent them. I was reminded of how important you have been in my life, Lord, and how happy I am to be a part of your family. What a wonderful part of your creation is the family of friends you have given us. You have made us need and rely on each other, and your Holy Spirit lives in each of us, even if some of us don't know it. You were present also at our celebration. It was a great time, wasn't it? Thank you Lord for this occasion, and for our family of friends.

Psalm 59

Heavenly Father and Creator, how wonderful

is
Your grace given so freely and abundantly.
You have anticipated our needs and desires
before we can feel and express them. What
an awesome provider you are. We need only
to look at Holy Scripture to find the answer
to questions that confound us. When aware
of your generosity and love, I have asked,
"What can I do to adequately respond to your
Gifts?"
Today I found in the writings of Paul what you
expect from us: It is to cling faithfully to the story
and truth of Jesus, and to pass on the message
of your love, grace and forgiveness. This is our
reason for being, is it not, Lord? What a joy it can
be.
Keep reminding me of this, Lord. I am so forgetful
and self-seeking, I need your constant presence to
keep me straight. Thank you Lord God for your
love.

Amen *Amen* *Amen*

Psalm 60

Lord God my creator, sustainer, and source of life, how great you are. You have provided for our every need before we have experienced it. You have filled our lives with what it takes to make us grow, and know
you better. You have provided us with teachers and leaders who know the things we need to know and show us the way. You have created a special class of people who dedicate their lives to this effort, and they are wonderful. We don't always appreciate them, and often treat them unkindly, but they persist in doing your work. Thank you Lord for these magnificent, special people, our Clergy. They are one of your best gifts.

Amen

Amen

Amen

Psalm 61

Lord God our Father in Heaven, something is wrong in my life, terribly wrong. Today I feel that you do not exist. The joy of your being beside me has been lost. I don't know what has happened to the security your presence brings. All of the cynical thoughts that enter my mind, which I can usually dismiss with a quick prayer, grow and multiply beyond reason. Even at worship service, I am bombarded with hopeless ideas, and evil thoughts. Where have you gone? How does the evil one get me so completely captured?
What can I do? I know you must still be available to rescue me from the grasp of the evil force that has engulfed me, but I can't find you. Please, Lord, bring me again the peace that only your presence can bring. I need help and I need it now.

Amen

Amen

Amen

Amen

Psalm 62

Lord God our father in Heaven in whose creation we live and prosper, we do have a problem. We are killing each other, stealing from each other, breaking all of your laws to satisfy our lust for money and power. We are doing horrible things to our children, even those of us who are avowed to teach Your way. What is wrong with us?

It looks as if your beautiful creation is being destroyed by those you love.

What can we do to save the world from this desecration?

What is going to happen to your magnificent work of beauty?

When You hung on the cross, You said You had overcome Evil. Why is it still so powerful? You are the power. Is the gain the evil one has made our fault? Has our part been left undone?

I think so; I think You have saved the world and what we need to do is introduce You to those that don't know you.

We need to go and tell, and start now.

Amen

Amen

Amen

Psalm 63

What can I say, Lord, after I say thank you? You are always there when I need you, you have never failed me. You are as close as you can be. All I need do is reach out to you and you respond and I learn again that you give hope where there is hopelessness, faith where there is faithlessness and fear. We are yours and you will not let us go. You love us so much that You died for us in one of the most painful and humiliating forms of execution known to man. Thank you, Lord Jesus.

Amen

Psalm 64

Lord God our creator, this is a sad day for me.

One of my good friends is dying.
We have been good friends for years.
My children and his grew up together, and I feel like his children are mine I am very sad because even though we have been very close, I know he does not know you or how much you love him. I feel like such a failure, since I have known for some time that he
was not a believer. My witness to him has been ineffective. His children are all believers, but he is not. Even though he Is aware of his impending demise, he shows no interest in
hearing the Good News, therefore I am praying for him.

Lord God our creator, I ask your blessing on my friend, and be gentle with him, because since he doesn't know You, he must be terribly frightened. I also pray that you will direct me in any way I can help. Lord have mercy on us,
Christ have mercy on us, Lord have mercy on us.

Amen Amen Amen Amen

Psalm 65

My Lord and Savior, this has been a great day, a day of victory for me. I was able to do a task this morning that I have been unable to do for years. Since the onset of Parkinson's Disease I have had difficulty performing some acts that required a coordinated use of both hands in small areas, as in buttoning my shirt,
or tying my shoestring. This morning I was waiting for my wife to help me button my top shirt button, which I have been unable to do for years. I always try, but am never successful.
This morning, however I did it, and it thrilled both of us. To be able to accomplish this simple act made me feel wonderful. It is not a very big achievement unless you are unable to do it, then it is a major achievement. And for this, Lord, I thank you, and praise your Holy Name.

Amen Amen Amen

Psalm 66

My Lord and God, it is that time in the Church year when we prepare for the celebration of the Resurrection of our
Lord Jesus. It is Ash Wednesday. As a symbol of our fidelity we have the priest place a bit of ashes on our forehead, before we receive Holy Eucharist. This causes a dilemma for some of
us in knowing what to do after we receive the ashes. If one wipes the ashes off at once, one could be considered insincere.
If one leaves the ashes on and goes back to work, one could be showing off, or worse, enjoying the notoriety. Jesus had some things to say about praying too loud in public, which were not very flattering. I wonder what he would say about our Ash Wednesday ritual.
Well, I got my ashes, then forgot about them and went to lunch where there were others with the mark on their forehead also. I wonder if they were showing off. I wonder if I was. Lord have mercy on us.

Amen Amen Amen

Psalm 67

My Lord God, when reading the Psalter I was impressed that David and the other psalmists were constantly in trouble.
They were always pleading with you to fight their battles, injure their adversaries, intercede for them, or they were thanking you for coming to their aid in some disaster they had created themselves I don't feel that the people in King David's time were much different from the way we are in the relationship we have with you. (We do have the Law Summary from Jesus, but that doesn't make things easier. It really makes the Law harder to obey. You not only must refrain from killing your enemy, you must love him.) Maybe they were more sensitive to your will. Perhaps we need to get closer to you, in order that we might see ourselves as You see us. We might find that we need more protection than we think. Lent will be an excellent time to have a look at how close we come to being the loving people that Jesus commanded us to be.

Amen Amen Amen

Psalm 68

Most holy God and Father, I have just reread the story about Abraham and his son Isaac. Now this is where you and I would
have a parting. I could not do what Abraham did; I just could not have done that. I have heard this story many times, and have admired Abraham for what he did, but have never put myself in his place so completely before, and I know I could not have done it. Does this mean that you love me more than I love you? I am sure it does, since you did it for me, and you didn't find a scapegoat to take your son's place. Wow, what a deal. How can one ignore a love like that? Too good to be true? Yes, but I believe it is true. I have a long way to go, and I had better get started.
Lord have mercy on me, a sinner.

Amen

Amen

Amen

Lord God my creator and counselor, we need to talk. Paul is quoted in Holy Scripture as saying, "I do not understand my own actions. For I do not do what I want, but I do the very thing that I hate." Now this is where Paul and I agree. This is certainly my nature, and it is comforting to know that St. Paul had the same problem. I know the law, your law, the civil law, and so far I have been able to stay out of jail. However if you had a police force I know that I would be in great trouble with them, especially if they could read my mind, and know my motivations. It is so easy to appear to be pious and good, yet have evil thoughts driving all one's action. I don't need any more rules or laws; what I need is a good lawyer, or better yet, what I need is a savior. Could it be that Jesus has that included in his good news? I am certainly counting on that.

Amen

My Lord God, and heavenly Father and creator,
You have done a wonderful thing for us. Your prophet Jeremiah has written, "I will put my law within them, I will write it on their hearts." This has always been a meaningful passage to me, but I have felt that I have never known its full meaning. Initially I had assumed that this was how our conscience was installed in our being. Now I feel that this is what you have done is to put Yourself into our being. I think mankind has had available your direction from the beginning, but the sinful action that man displays rather than the wholesome, loving nature that you intended for us to display comes from a misdirection of that gift. We have just enough of you in us to make us want to be god, rather than your person. When Jesus lived he showed us how to listen to and obey your messages, but we didn't like that, it was too hard. So we killed him. But he didn't stay dead, He came at us with another deal. He said love one another, as I love you. Better than that, just believe that I am who I claim to be, and stay close to me, and that will make me happy and not only give you eternal life starting now but I

will be with you from now on. For this I give you thanks and praise.

Amen

Amen

Amen

Amen

Psalm 71

Lord God, my creator and heavenly father,

Lord Jesus, my savior and friend, Lord Holy Spirit, my comforter and guide, what a wonderful gift you have given me in my life. To be alive and to know you and to know that I am a part of your creation is a gift beyond all imagination. For this I praise Your Holy Name.

For Holy Scripture, and those ancients who lived and recorded their relationship with you, and the Prophets who tried to restore that relationship when they would go astray, I thank you and praise Your Holy Name.

For the ancient Church, imperfect as it was, which kept alive the story, and spoke for you over the centuries and made known to all the world your love for us, I thank you and praise Your Holy Name.

For my parents, grandparents, and all my ancestors who knew you and passed on your story that I might know you and your love for all of us, and especially me, I thank you and praiseYour Holy Name.

For my birth into this world to a loving family who knew You and taught me the story about your love for us, which has made my life so wonderful, I thank you and praise Your Holy Name.

For my childhood in a community of God lovers, which made loving you a normal and accepted thing to do, even though much of my behavior would not suggest that I knew you, I thank you and praise Your Holy Name

For the opportunity to serve my country and seeing me safely through naval engagements and a typhoon, and bringing me home to a loving and grateful community, I thank you and praise Your Holy Name.

For convincing the love of my life that I had more potential than my past history would indicate, and directing me to pursue and consummate that love, I really do thank you and praise Your Holy Name.

For guiding me to the study of medicine and for staying with me through the course of that study, and allowing me to learn about the wonderful body you have given us, I thank you and praise Your Holy Name.

For two beautiful daughters who have provided us with two wonderful sons and three magnificent granddaughters as well as many unforgettable memories, I do indeed thank you and praise Your Holy Name.

For over forty five years of medical practice during which I have had the privilege to serve many beautiful patients, delivering babies, fixing fractures, treating medical and surgical problems, I thank you and praise Your Holy Name.

For the gift of laughter, music, good books, delicious food and drinks, and outstanding friends to share them with; for a community who love and worship You, I thank you and praise Your Holy Name.

For the opportunity to serve your Church as a layman in many capacities, to learn more about you from the outstanding clergy, and become part of a marvelous Church family, I thank you and praise Your Holy Name.

For allowing me to personally experience first hand your healing ability of coronary heart disease, colon cancer and Parkinson's Disease, I thank you and praise Your Holy Name.

For the opportunity to learn for myself what it is to be an old person, and yet feel the excitement of a young Church growing closer to you, and becoming the family You want us to be, I thank you and praise Your Holy Name.

For the days I have left in this wonderful world, and the knowledge that you are really there, and here beside me, and will be beside me forever, I thank you and praise Your Holy Name forever.

Alleluia,

Alleluia,

Alleluia.

Amen

THE END